P9-CBR-559

Reporter for the World

NELLIE BLY

Martha E. Kendall

The Millbrook Press
Brookfield, Connecticut
A Gateway Biography

Cover photograph courtesy of The Bettmann Archive,
hand coloring by North Wind Pictures

Background photograph courtesy of New York Public Library,
Newspaper Collection, Astor, Lenox, and Tilden Foundations.

Photographs courtesy of UPI/Bettmann: pp. 4, 41 (bottom),
42; The Bettmann Archive: pp. 8 (both), 17, 24, 27, 30, 36;
Library of Congress: p. 11; Culver Pictures: pp. 14, 20;
Foster Hall Memorial, University of Pittsburgh: p. 19; New
York Public Library, Newspaper Collection, Astor, Lenox, and
Tilden Foundations: pp. 32, 35; The Museum of the City of
New York: p. 39; Carnegie Library of Pittsburgh: p. 41 (top).

Library of Congress Cataloging-in-Publication Data

Kendall, Martha E., 1947–
Nellie Bly : reporter for the world / by Martha E. Kendall.

p.   cm. — (A Gateway biography)
Includes bibliographical references and index.
Summary: a biography of a woman whose exposé of the insane
asylums in New York City in the late 1800s was the beginning
of her journalistic career.
ISBN 1–56294–061–9 ISBN 1-56294-787-7 (pbk.)
1. Bly, Nellie, 1867–1922—Juvenile literature. 2. Journalists—
United States—Biography—Juvenile literature. [1. Bly, Nellie,
1867–1922. 2. Journalists.] I. Title. II Series.
PN4874.C59K4   1992
070′.92—dc20
[B]   91–37643   CIP   AC

Nellie Bly

Nellie Bly, whose real name was Elizabeth Cochrane, became famous as a newspaper reporter. Her stories helped improve many people's lives.

If Elizabeth Cochrane made up her mind to do something, she did it.

As a young woman in 1887, she was having trouble finding a job, even though she looked and looked for one. Then somebody stole her purse! She had almost no money left. She had to come up with an idea, fast.

Elizabeth was determined that she *would* get a job, no matter what. And it would be the job she wanted—as a reporter at the *World,* the most exciting newspaper in New York City. Owned by Joseph Pulitzer, the newspaper was famous for covering subjects important not just to rich people, but to all people.

Elizabeth feared that no newspaper in New York City wanted to hire a woman. But that would not stop her. She set out to conquer the *World.*

At first, the guard at the *World*'s office would not even let Elizabeth in to see Mr. Pulitzer. But she did not give up. She waited. And waited. And waited. She would not leave. After many hours she managed to speak with the editor, John Cockerill, who was impressed by her determination. Finally he and Mr. Pulitzer listened to her ideas for newspaper stories. They agreed to let her try the most exciting one. If she succeeded, she would be hired by the *World.* In the meantime, they gave her twenty-five dollars and wished her luck.

Elizabeth's idea was to pretend she was crazy!

Many people in New York wondered what went on at Blackwell's Island. It was a place for poor women who had been judged insane. If they did not have money to pay for treatment to get better, they were sent to the island. The women did not want to go. And once there, they almost never came back.

Using the name Nellie Brown, Elizabeth planned to pretend she was insane and poor. Unlike any other woman in that situation, she *did* hope to be taken to Blackwell's Island. She wanted to see for herself what happened to women there. The *World* promised to get her off the island after ten days had passed. Then she would write about her experience.

Nervous and excited, Elizabeth began her crazy adventure. With seventy-three cents in her pocket, she got a room at a cheap boardinghouse for women. She wanted the people there to think she was insane. She stared at the other women and spoke little. Then she claimed she was from Cuba, and she was waiting for her suitcase to arrive. Again and again she cried that everything was very sad. She said she was afraid of crazy people and that everyone there looked crazy! By the end of the night, the people at the boardinghouse felt that Nellie Brown was truly insane.

In the morning Nellie refused to leave, and the police were called. Next, a judge and several doctors talked with her. They agreed that she must go to Blackwell's Island. Elizabeth's plan was working perfectly.

Once she got to the island, she discovered that her suspicions about the place were true. Like prisoners, the women were locked in. The nurses said mean things, if they paid the women any attention at all. Even worse, the so-called doctors did nothing to help their patients. Elizabeth stopped acting crazy as soon as she arrived on the island, but the doctors did not listen to her. Elizabeth felt sure that many of the women were just as sane as she was, but that made no difference to these doctors.

Above: The hospital at Blackwell's Island, in New York City.

Below: At Blackwell's Island, patients were crowded together and often neglected.

Elizabeth and the other women were not given enough clothes or blankets to keep warm. For baths, the attendants poured buckets of cold water over the women's heads. When that was done to her, Elizabeth felt as if she would really go crazy!

After she had been on the island for ten days, Elizabeth was relieved when the *World* arranged for her release. She wrote about her experience, describing Blackwell's Island as a "human rat-trap. It is easy to get in, but once there it is impossible to get out." She said the cruel treatment there could make a healthy person go insane.

Her story made many people in New York angry. They demanded reform. As a result of Elizabeth's work, she was pleased to report that the city spent one million dollars more per year than ever before to improve the treatment of the insane.

Elizabeth's story was a success. People bought the paper just to read what she had written. Mr. Pulitzer was satisfied, and he hired Elizabeth as a reporter for the *World.* Of course, in the newspaper she was not called Elizabeth Cochrane. By this time she was known as Nellie Bly. And how she got that name is another story.

On May 5, 1865, Mary Jane and Michael Cochran added another child to their large family. They named her Elizabeth, never dreaming that the world would come to know her as Nellie Bly.

Perhaps it was from her father that Elizabeth learned to be so determined. He had been a poor laborer in a mill in the town of Pitts Mills, Pennsylvania. He worked hard and saved his money. Then he bought the mill. After that, he bought more and more land. He ran the post office, as well as many of the local businesses. Finally, he changed the name of the town to honor its wealthiest citizen— himself! Pitts Mills became known as Cochran's Mills. And that's where Elizabeth was born.

She grew to be a slim, pretty girl with curly brown hair and twinkling hazel eyes. Even though she was small, she was lively, determined, and used to getting her own way. Her favorite color was pink. She wore pink so often that her nickname at home became Pinky.

In 1869 the Cochran family moved from Cochran's Mills to nearby Apollo, where Elizabeth's father became a lawyer and then a judge. He had

Elizabeth was a lively girl who liked to read and play games with her brothers.

many books in his library, and he encouraged his children to read. But then Elizabeth's father died. He left the family plenty of money to live on—at least for a while.

Girls in the 1870s usually spent most of their time at home cooking, cleaning, and doing housework. But none of these things interested Elizabeth. Instead, she loved to read books and write stories. She also wanted to do all the things her older brothers did. She spent many afternoons outside playing with them. When she got tired of their games, she dreamed about her mother's Uncle Thomas Kennedy. He had traveled around the world. The family loved to tell about Uncle Thomas's trip, which lasted three years. He had planned to write a book about it when he returned, but his health was poor, and he did not get it written. Uncle Thomas never could have guessed that one day a family member *would* write a book about a trip around the world. And of course no one could have predicted the many adventures that Elizabeth Cochran would grow up to have.

After Elizabeth's older brothers had married and moved away, Elizabeth, her mother, and her younger sister left Apollo and settled in Pittsburgh, Pennsylvania.

There she found that the main concern of most of her friends was finding a husband. But not Elizabeth! She wanted to do something exciting. However, she found little excitement in Pittsburgh. Instead, she found that the money her father had left his family was almost gone. Now they needed money, and Elizabeth wanted to work.

Employers in Pittsburgh did not care about what Elizabeth wanted. Every day she looked for a good job, but she could not find one. She read the newspaper, hoping she might see an ad for an exciting position that would pay enough to support her and her family. But she could find nothing.

Then, one day in January 1885, Elizabeth happened to read something that made her really mad. It was an article in Pittsburgh's newspaper, the *Dispatch.* The story was called "What Girls Are Good For." It made fun of girls who tried to do things that many men had always been able to do—things like earn good pay for doing interesting work, or be allowed to vote. Pinky's face turned pink with anger. She sat down and wrote to the

Pittsburgh was a growing city in the 1880s.

Dispatch. She said that some women needed to work to support their families, but few jobs were open to them, and the pay was terrible. She claimed that women could do many things—and do them well—if only they were given the chance.

The men at the *Dispatch* were so impressed by Elizabeth's letter that they *did* give her a chance. They advertised in the paper that they wanted to know who wrote that letter, which Elizabeth had left unsigned. Elizabeth responded in writing, and the editors of the *Dispatch* suggested she do another article. They invited their new writer to come to the office so that they could meet her in person. Surely they expected to see a bitter old woman, or a man who had written from a woman's point of view. What a surprise when pretty young Elizabeth, not yet twenty years old, introduced herself to them!

They offered Elizabeth a job, with good pay. She could not have been any happier, for she had found work doing what she loved best—writing!

She chose to do her next article on the shocking topic of divorce. In the 1880s, even though many marriages were unhappy, divorce was not common. Few people talked about the subject. But Elizabeth knew something about divorce, for her mother had divorced the man she married after Elizabeth's father had died. In her article, Elizabeth described unhappy homes, mean husbands, and bad wives. She said one big problem was that very few women could get good jobs. They saw marriage as their only choice, even if they couldn't find a man they loved.

Elizabeth wrote that it was better for people *not* to get married unless they really wanted to. Then more marriages would be happy, and few divorces would be needed. The editors at the *Dispatch* liked the article, and they said it would be published as soon as Elizabeth got a new name.

In those days, newspaper writers used a "pen name." That's a made-up name for authors. Elizabeth already knew that names were important. To make her name special, she had started writing an extra *e* on the end of it: Cochrane. But for her newspaper stories she needed a totally different name, one that was catchy and easy to remember.

When Elizabeth and one of the editors were sitting at his desk trying to think of a pen name for

A scene from a divorce court in the 1880s. When Elizabeth wrote her story for the Dispatch, *divorce was thought to be scandalous.*

her, an assistant walked by. He was humming a popular tune—Stephen Foster's song "Nelly Bly." Perfect! The article on divorce was published, under the byline "Nellie Bly."

The readers of the *Dispatch* liked what Nellie Bly had to say, and the newspaper owners were pleased because they sold many newspapers.

People in Pittsburgh tried to guess who the *Dispatch*'s new reporter was. Many people thought that "Nellie Bly" *must* be a man. They said few ladies dared even to mention divorce, much less write about it as strongly as Nellie Bly had. But while readers wondered who Nellie Bly might be, Elizabeth decided on a topic for a new series of articles—working women.

To get information, Elizabeth introduced herself to the owner of a large bottle-making factory. Dressed as a proper young lady, she spoke very politely to him. She said she wanted to write a story for the *Dispatch* about the women who worked in his factory. He liked the attention and agreed to let her visit. He had no idea that this reporter would

Elizabeth took her pen name from a popular song by Stephen Foster. A printer changed the spelling from "Nelly" to "Nellie."

In the late 1800s, women worked long hours for little pay in factories such as this.

grow famous for letting the truth be known about terrible factories like his!

Elizabeth suspected that conditions in his factory might be bad, but she was shocked to find out just how bad they were. In the winter, workers had to wrap rags around their feet to keep their toes from freezing. For fourteen hours a day, they stood up on the hard cement floor. And the place was dirty! Elizabeth thought she saw almost as many rats as people there.

The work was dangerous, too, for bottles often broke. And most women were paid less than half what the men earned! Seeing how these women suffered made Elizabeth really mad. She wrote in detail about the factory's conditions. Nellie Bly's articles shocked the readers of the *Dispatch*. But Elizabeth felt she still had not done enough. To know the full truth about something, she wanted to experience it for herself. Elizabeth decided to act the part of a factory worker. Then she would write about what happened to her.

She dressed like a poor working woman. With little trouble, she got a job making copper cables. She worked in a dark basement, and her eyes hurt from trying to see what she was doing. Even though she was strong and healthy, her back ached from leaning over for hours. She was not allowed to pause for a moment. And then Elizabeth was fired! Why? Because she got a drink of water without asking the foreman for permission!

Luckily for Elizabeth, her real job was writing, not working in that terrible shop. In the *Dispatch*, she described her experience. She wrote that many working women—and some children—suffered under such conditions every day.

The people of Pittsburgh were angry when they read Nellie Bly's story. They insisted that women in factories get better treatment.

The *Dispatch* was very happy with their new reporter. More and more people wanted to buy the newspaper so they could read her stories. But the owners of the factories did not like the way Nellie Bly made them look like cruel bosses. They told the *Dispatch* that they were so mad about what Nellie Bly wrote that they might stop advertising in the newspaper. The *Dispatch* could not afford that.

So Elizabeth was given other subjects to write about. She interviewed important people and covered general city news. But Elizabeth had not changed. She still wanted excitement in her life. And she had another idea.

Elizabeth wanted the men who ran the *Dispatch* to send her to Mexico. Readers were curious to know about this neighbor south of the United States. About twenty years had passed since the Mexican Revolution, and Americans wondered what that country was like now. How did Mexicans live? What did they eat? What did they do for fun? Nellie Bly would be more than happy to find out.

The men at the *Dispatch* worried about their "girl reporter." She was only twenty-one years old. They did not think she would be safe in Mexico. They said she could not go. But Elizabeth refused to take no for an answer. She was determined to persuade the editors to let her go—and, finally, she did. She invited her mother to travel with her, and in 1886 they headed west.

Once she got to Mexico, Elizabeth learned Spanish fast. She met lots of people and traveled around the country. She visited the big old churches, admired the colorful clothes of the peasants, and loved the elegant dresses of the rich

A market square in Mexico. Elizabeth's stories gave many of her readers their first glimpse of life in that country.

women. She ate the spicy food. Then she sent recipes to the *Dispatch,* so that people in Pittsburgh who were daring enough could try them.

Nellie Bly described the beauty and history of Mexico, but she also wrote about things she did not like. For example, some Mexican newspaper reporters had published information about bad things the government did. As a result, the reporters were sent to jail. Very angry about this injustice, Elizabeth wrote an article for American newspapers describing what had happened. Government leaders in Mexico saw her article, and they were not happy about it. They thought Nellie Bly was a troublemaker. She had to leave the country.

Elizabeth began her trip home, but she worried—would her stories about Mexico be taken from her? She watched nervously when the inspector at the Mexican border searched her suitcases. Elizabeth pointed to one and said it contained her underwear. Embarrassed, the inspector did not open that case. But really her newspaper stories were hidden in it! Both Elizabeth and her stories safely crossed the border and made it to Pittsburgh.

Elizabeth's stories were very popular, and the

Dispatch gave her a big raise. But Elizabeth wanted more than money. She wanted challenges and adventures. In 1887 she headed for the center of the publishing industry, New York City.

It was in New York that Elizabeth had her "crazy" adventure—she acted insane and wrote about what happened to her on Blackwell's Island. Her story was so good that Joseph Pulitzer hired her for his famous newspaper, the *World.*

Elizabeth went on to play more roles to find out the truth for her stories. Readers looked forward to Nellie Bly's stories, unaware that the most exciting one was yet to come. Elizabeth had a new idea—a very big idea.

One of Elizabeth's favorite books was *Around the World in Eighty Days* by the French author Jules Verne. It was about Phileas Fogg, a man who made a bet. He claimed he could travel around the world in eighty days, which was considered a very short time. There were no cars or airplanes then. People traveled on slow trains and slow boats, which often did not leave or arrive on time. In the

Joseph Pulitzer, who hired Elizabeth to write for the World.

book, no one thought Phileas Fogg could make such a fast trip. But he won his bet, traveling all the way around the world in eighty days.

Elizabeth's idea was to try to beat Phileas Fogg's record. Of course, his trip never really happened. It was a story made up by Jules Verne. But Elizabeth thought she could do the trip. And she also thought the readers of the *World* would like to hear about her adventures.

The men at the *World* loved the idea—but they said Elizabeth could not go. They claimed that a woman would not be safe traveling alone. They also said that a woman needed many trunks full of clothes and hats and shoes, more than she could carry by herself. Trying to make fast connections between trains and boats would be impossible with so much luggage.

So they decided to send a man on the trip!

Elizabeth couldn't believe her ears. After all, it was *her* idea! She said that if they sent a man, she would quit writing for the *World.* She would find another newspaper that would send her. And she would beat the man from the *World!*

By this time, the editors at the paper knew

Elizabeth well. If she made up her mind to do something, she would do it. They talked it over with Joseph Pulitzer himself, and he approved her trip. In a matter of days, she was ready to go.

Elizabeth bought a warm blue wool outfit. Then she got a new coat, a long plaid one called an Ulster. With a raincoat and a hat, her clothes were all set. She packed everything into a very small suitcase called a gripsack.

On the morning of November 14, 1889, she began her trip. She boarded a ship, the *Augusta Victoria*, to England. She planned to write about everything that happened to her, and to cable her stories back to New York.

When Elizabeth got to England, she learned that Jules Verne, author of *Around the World in Eighty Days*, wanted to meet her. She was thrilled. But she wondered—could she afford the time to travel to France where he lived? She had to beat Phileas Fogg's record, and every day counted.

She decided to go. When they met, Jules Verne was charmed by this daring young reporter. However, he doubted that she could go around the world faster than his character Phileas Fogg did. If

*Elizabeth in her
Ulster coat,
ready to travel
around the world.
She carried
everything she
needed in a
small gripsack.*

she succeeded, he said, he would be very happy for her. He wished her luck.

Elizabeth hurried along. Her next stop was in Italy. When she tried to send a cable back to the *World* to tell the readers about her progress, she found that the cable operator had never even heard of New York City!

For the first three weeks of her trip, readers anxiously waited to find out what had become of Nellie Bly. They could only guess and worry about her, because it took twenty-four long days for her first article to arrive at the *World*.

On her ship to Egypt, Elizabeth met many interesting people. And they thought *she* was interesting, too. In fact, two men proposed to her. But she refused—getting married was the last thing on her mind. She was thinking about Phileas Fogg and his eighty-day trip.

From Egypt, she traveled to Ceylon. There she waited five long days for a ship to Singapore, where she finally fell in love. With who? A monkey! He kept her good company, but between Singapore and Hong Kong her ship went through a terrible storm. Then the superstitious sailors claimed the

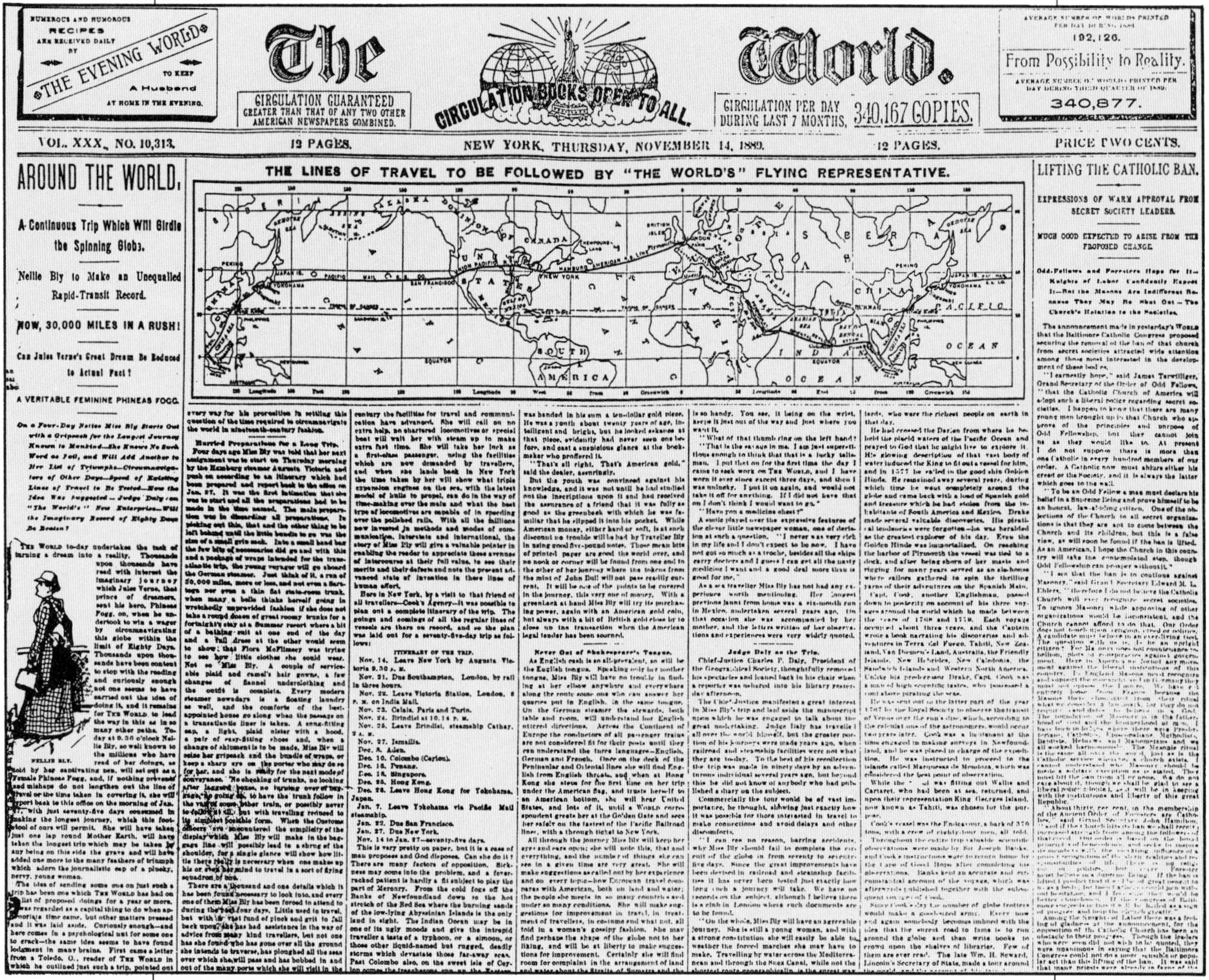

HUMOROUS AND HUMOROUS RECIPES ARE RECEIVED DAILY BY THE EVENING WORLD TO KEEP A Husband AT HOME IN THE EVENING.

The World.

CIRCULATION GUARANTEED GREATER THAN THAT OF ANY TWO OTHER AMERICAN NEWSPAPERS COMBINED.

CIRCULATION BOOKS OPEN TO ALL.

CIRCULATION PER DAY DURING LAST 7 MONTHS, 340,167 COPIES.

192,126.

From Possibility to Reality.

340,877.

VOL. XXX., NO. 10,313. 12 PAGES. NEW YORK, THURSDAY, NOVEMBER 14, 1889. 12 PAGES. PRICE TWO CENTS.

AROUND THE WORLD.

A Continuous Trip Which Will Girdle the Spinning Globe.

Nellie Bly to Make an Unequalled Rapid-Transit Record.

NOW, 30,000 MILES IN A RUSH!

Can Jules Verne's Great Dream Be Reduced to Actual Fact?

A VERITABLE FEMININE PHINEAS FOGG.

THE LINES OF TRAVEL TO BE FOLLOWED BY "THE WORLD'S" FLYING REPRESENTATIVE.

NELLIE BLY.

ITINERARY OF THE TRIP.

Nov. 14. Leave New York by Augusta Victoria 9.30 A. M.

Nov. 21. Due Southampton, London, by rail in three hours.

Nov. 22. Leave Victoria Station, London, 8 P. M. on India Mail.

Nov. 23. Calais, Paris and Turin.

Nov. 24. Brindisi at 10.14 P. M.

Nov. 25. Leave Brindisi, steamship Cathay.

Nov. 27. Ismailia.

Dec. 3. Aden.

Dec. 10. Colombo (Ceylon).

Dec. 16. Penang.

Dec. 18. Singapore.

Dec. 25. Hong Kong.

Dec. 28. Leave Hong Kong for Yokohama, Japan.

Jan. 7. Leave Yokohama via Pacific Mail steamship.

Jan. 22. Due San Francisco.

Jan. 27. Due New York.

Nov. 14 to Jan. 27—seventy-five days.

Never Out of Shakespeare's Tongue.

Judge Daly on the Trip.

LIFTING THE CATHOLIC BAN.

EXPRESSIONS OF WARM APPROVAL FROM SECRET SOCIETY LEADERS.

MUCH GOOD EXPECTED TO ARISE FROM THE PROPOSED CHANGE.

The front page of the World *on the day Elizabeth set off.*

monkey brought bad luck, and they wanted Elizabeth to throw him overboard. She held tight to him, and soon the weather cleared up.

A different kind of storm was waiting for her in Hong Kong. There she was told that another woman was racing her around the world! Her name was Elizabeth Bisland, and she was an editor of *Cosmopolitan* magazine. She had left New York the same day Nellie Bly had. Elizabeth Bisland had already passed through Hong Kong. Traveling in the opposite direction, she was trying to beat Nellie Bly. And she was making excellent time.

What if someone else won the race?

Elizabeth felt helpless. There were no boats leaving Hong Kong for five more days. She was losing precious time. Finally, she boarded a ship bound for Japan.

From there she crossed the Pacific on the *Oceanic*. By this point in her trip, Nellie Bly was famous. The captain of the ship wrote a sign in the engine room:

> FOR NELLIE BLY
> WE'LL WIN OR DIE

But a problem developed right before they landed in San Francisco. To get off the ship, all the passengers needed papers from a doctor saying that they were healthy and would not bring any sickness into America. By mistake, the papers had been left in Japan. It would take two weeks to get them. Desperate to get to shore faster, Elizabeth threatened to jump overboard and swim in by herself.

Before she actually jumped into the water, a doctor was called. He looked at the passengers to see if they were healthy. Then a tugboat carried Elizabeth to shore ahead of the rest of the people. But the doctor called to her that he had forgotten to check her tongue. Waving and laughing as her tugboat pulled away from the ship, she stuck her tongue out at the doctor!

Crowds of people greeted Nellie Bly in San Francisco. But of course she did not stay there long. She had only one week left to make it all the way across the United States. Now that she was this close, she couldn't let anything prevent her from winning the race. But she did make many very short stops on her train ride from San Francisco to Jersey City, New Jersey. Crowds jammed the train

While Elizabeth traveled, the World *promoted her trip with games and contests.*

A huge crowd turned out to greet
Nellie Bly at the end of her trip.

stations, bands played pieces composed in her honor, and well-wishers gave her flowers, food, clothes, souvenirs, and jewelry. The country felt very proud of their young American girl!

On January 26, 1890, Nellie Bly arrived in Jersey City, the final train station of her trip. It was the seventy-second day of her journey. Thousands of cheering people greeted her. The headline of the *World* exclaimed, "Father Time Outdone!"

Almost a million people had entered a contest guessing exactly when she would finish her trip. The winner, F. W. Stevens, came within two seconds of her arrival time. His prize was a free trip to Europe—but at a leisurely pace. At her fast pace, Elizabeth had set a new world record. Jules Verne sent her a telegram with his congratulations.

The little monkey that had traveled with Elizabeth from Singapore all the way to America found life in her New York City apartment to be too confining. Elizabeth realized he could not stay with her there, so she gave him away to the Central Park Zoo.

And what happened to Elizabeth Bisland, the woman who tried to beat Nellie Bly? She did complete her trip, but it took her four days longer. She never became famous.

Only *three years before,* Elizabeth had been a poor young woman without a dime in her purse. In fact, she did not even have a purse, because a thief had stolen it! By 1890, she had earned both fame and fortune. Her name was used in songs, ads, and pictures, and Nellie Bly coats and hats became the popular fashion for women. Elizabeth wrote a best-seller, called *Nellie Bly's Book: Around the World in 72 Days.* She was invited to speak in many places, so that people could see and hear the adventurous Nellie Bly. Her $25,000 salary was probably the highest of any reporter in the country.

Although Elizabeth enjoyed life as a well-paid celebrity, she decided to take a break from her busy schedule. She left the *World* and sampled the luxuries her money could buy. But after a few years away from the newspaper, Elizabeth felt bored.

In 1893 she went back to the *World* as a reporter with her own column. In order to get information for her stories, she traveled a great deal.

NELLIE BLY BIDS FOGG GOOD BYE.

O Fogg, good bye", said Nellie Bly.
"It takes a maiden to be spry,
to span the space twixt thought and act.
And turn a fiction to a fact".

Many advertisements featured Nellie Bly's adventures. This one, for a patent medicine, shows her waving good-bye to Phileas Fogg, the main character of the novel Around the World in Eighty Days.

On a train to Chicago in the spring of 1895, she met someone who changed her life. Elizabeth fell in love, but this time it was not with a little monkey in Singapore! Only a few days after their meeting, she married Robert L. Seaman. At 72 he was much older than Elizabeth, who was only 29. He was a millionaire banker and businessman, and some people claimed Elizabeth wanted his money. But she was already rich from her earnings as a reporter. She paid no attention to what people said.

Seaman died in 1904, after he and Elizabeth had been married for nine years. Elizabeth took over one of his companies, called Iron Clad Manufacturing. Remembering the terrible conditions in Pittsburgh's factories that she had seen years before, she made sure workers were treated well in her factory. She paid men and women equally, and they all got family health care. Elizabeth created another successful business, the American Steel Barrel Company.

Then troubles began. Another company stole some of her designs. A fire destroyed much of Iron Clad Manufacturing. Too late, Elizabeth discovered that her managers had taken much of her

THE IRON CLAD FACTORIES
ARE THE LARGEST

Of their kind and are owned exclusively
by

☀ NELLIE BLY ☀

The only woman in the world
personally managing
Industries of such a magnitude

NATIONAL BOTTLERS' CONVENTION
CLEVELAND, OHIO
OCTOBER 15, 16 and 17, 1901

Above: An advertisement for Iron Clad Manufacturing, Elizabeth's company. Right: As a reporter during World War I, Elizabeth chats with an Austrian army officer.

Elizabeth (right) used her column in the Evening Journal *to help working women and poor children.*

company's money. In 1914 she told her lawyers to settle things for her. She went to Austria to visit friends and get away from her worries.

While she was in Austria, World War I began. Austria refused to let any Americans leave. What could Elizabeth do? She decided to return to what she did best—writing newspaper stories. She was the first woman correspondent in the war.

When the war ended, Elizabeth returned home. One of the editors at the New York *Evening Journal* invited Elizabeth to write a column for his paper. She accepted. She used her column to help the homeless children of New York. Nellie Bly explained to her readers that these children had nowhere warm to sleep, ate food from garbage cans, and had no families. She helped many of them find good homes.

In early January 1922, Elizabeth caught pneumonia. She died on January 27 at age 56. The *Evening Journal* wrote: "She was the best reporter in America."

Many people's lives improved thanks to the courage, honesty, and determination of Elizabeth Cochrane Seaman—the one and only Nellie Bly.

Important Dates

May 5, 1865	Elizabeth Cochran is born in Cochran's Mills, Pennsylvania.
1885	Hired by the Pittsburgh *Dispatch*, where she adopts the byline "Nellie Bly."
1886	Spends six months in Mexico and sends stories to the *Dispatch*.
1887	Moves to New York City; hired by Joseph Pulitzer's *World*.
November 14, 1889–January 26, 1890	Makes her record-breaking trip around the world.
1895	Marries Robert Seaman.
1904	Seaman dies; Elizabeth takes over the management of his business.
1914	Becomes a news correspondent during World War I.
1919	Returns to New York and writes for the *Evening Journal* on the needs of homeless children.
January 27, 1922	Dies of pneumonia in New York.

Further Reading

Around the World in Eighty Days. Jules Verne (Bantam, 1984). Advanced readers may enjoy this novel, which inspired Nellie Bly's trip around the world.

Ida Tarbell: Pioneer Woman Journalist and Biographer. Adrian A. Paradis (Childrens Press, 1985). Ida Tarbell was another important writer who lived at about the same time as Nellie Bly.

Making Headlines. Kathy Lynn Emerson (Dillon, 1989).

Nellie Bly, Reporter. Nina Brown Baker (Holt, Rinehart & Winston, 1956).

Index

Page numbers in *italics* refer to illustrations.